HIDDEN CHILD

HIDDEN CHILD

ISAAC MILLMAN

FRANCES FOSTER BOOKS

Farrar, Straus and Giroux

New York

In memory of
Héna Sztulman,
my mother and father, Moïshé and Rivelé Sztrymfman,
Léon and Élise Sztulman,
my paternal grandparents, Feiwel and Rachel Sztrymfman,
Uncle Hershel and Aunt Feige, and their sister whose name is
lost to memory,
my maternal grandparents, Yosef and Bina Fuchtel,
Uncles Abbe, Yakov, and Izak,
and my cousin Yvette Nisenman.
Hidden Child is also dedicated to my cousin
Joseph Nisenman

Héna and me, 1948

HIDDEN CHILD

Approximately 1,200,000 Jewish children
were deported and murdered by the Nazis and
their collaborators in the Holocaust of World War II.
Most of those who survived did so by being
sent into hiding. Some were hidden with other Jews.
Some went to convents and monasteries;
others were hidden on farms or taken in
by non-Jewish families and individuals.
My name is Isaac Sztrymfman,
and I was a hidden child.

Me, winter of 1936

Me, at the age of six

Me, on Marcel's back, in the playground before the war

Papa and I take home Mama's roast chicken

Mama, Papa, and me in Paris in 1938

The German army parades down the Champs-Élysées

We lived at 60, rue de la Fontaine au Roi

Eating herring at the Café Laumière with Papa

Mama, Papa, and me, persecuted for being Jews during the war

Me in the country, summer of 1939

BEFORE THE WAR

I crawled into Mama and Papa's bed and snuggled between them. "Good morning, Isaac," Mama whispered. "Don't wake up Papa. It's Sunday." That meant my father, who was a tailor, wouldn't be going to his shop that day. "I'll be very quiet," I whispered back. Mama kissed me and got up. I lay very still, not moving a muscle, until Papa opened his eyes. Then we stayed in bed a little longer, listening to Mama in the kitchen.

Mama had prepared breakfast and was now busy with the chicken she'd bought the day before. It was in an earthenware baking dish, and she was rubbing oil and garlic over its pinkish skin. She peeled small potatoes and placed them around the plucked chicken, then draped a linen towel over the dish.

"I'm taking Isaac with me!" Papa announced after breakfast as he took the chicken from Mama. "Well, don't be late," said Mama. "We won't," he answered. Mama laughed because she knew we would be.

Every Sunday, Papa and I followed the same routine. First we left the chicken to be roasted at the corner bakery because we didn't have an oven at home, just a gas range. Then we walked to the Café Laumière, where Papa's friends gathered. The café was crowded with customers speaking Yiddish, the language Mama and Papa spoke at home. Papa and his friends liked to talk, mostly about politics, and the discussions often got heated and loud.

Papa would forget about the time, and then we'd have to leave in a big hurry to pick up the chicken before the baker closed for lunch. In the afternoon, we would get dressed in our Sunday clothes and go visiting.

Mama and Papa and many of their friends had emigrated from Poland to France. Life was hard in Poland, especially for Jews. Papa, like many political idealists at that time, was a Communist and had spent a year in a Polish jail. In France, he didn't have to hide his Jewishness or his political convictions. I loved going to political rallies with him at La Place de la République on weekends. My friends were there, too. We raced in and out of the crowd on our roller skates while our dads listened to the long, boring speeches.

Our family was happy in Paris. We lived on the second floor of a six-story apartment building at 60, rue de la Fontaine au Roi, near La Place de la République. It was a neighborhood filled with Jewish immigrants. Many, like Papa, worked in the garment trade.

My friend Marcel Rosenbloom lived on the fifth floor of our apartment house. When Papa and Mama went out for the evening, I'd go up to the Rosenblooms' to play with Marcel. The green pillows from their living-room sofa became our battleships. We'd slide on the shiny parquet floor astride our pillows and attack each other. "My sub got yours!" "I sank your destroyer!" That was as close as war came to us then. It was a game.

GERMANY INVADES FRANCE

In 1940, the German army invaded France, and life under German occupation began. I was seven years old. Papa had to go to the police station and register us as Jews. Soon the government began imposing restrictions on Jews. When Papa came home one afternoon in 1941, he looked worried. He said that some of his Jewish friends had been arrested.

I began having nightmares. One night I dreamed that the police broke down our front door and dragged Mama and Papa away, leaving me behind. I told Mama about the nightmare. "Isaac," she said, trying to comfort me, "it's just a bad dream."

Not long after, Papa was ordered to report to the police station. That night, he took his green corduroy golf trousers and laid them out neatly with his gray striped jacket, brown cap, and Sunday shoes, as if he was getting ready for an important meeting. He tucked me in bed and kissed me tenderly. "Isaac, be a good boy, and help your mama!" In the morning, he was gone.

Soon, we received a letter from Papa. He was in an internment camp in a place called Pithiviers. A photograph accompanied the letter. "Mama, here's Papa!" I exclaimed, pointing him out. "And Cousin Joseph!" Mama added. Papa wrote that Joseph and several friends from Poland were there with him. The commander of the camp had given special permission for relatives to visit the following Sunday.

On June 22, 1940, France is divided into two zones. The Germans control the northern part of the country and the Vichy government administers the free zone in the south

⬡🏠 Principal camps where Jews were interned

🏳️🏠 Other camps where Jews were interned

▬ Area occupied by Germans

▬ Free French zone

▬ Line of demarcation

Compiègne   Drancy

Paris •

Pithiviers

Beaune-la-Rolande

Angers

Papa's and Mama's identification cards, stamped "Juif" and "Juive," meaning Jew

PITHIVIERS

Mama and I left our apartment before sunrise Sunday morning. The streets were deserted as we walked to the Métro at La Place de la République for the short subway ride to the bus station.

We boarded the crowded bus for the three-hour ride to Pithiviers and found seats together. It soon became obvious that most of the passengers on the bus were Jewish families, all going to the same place. I huddled against Mama, shut my eyes, and awoke as the bus pulled into Pithiviers. We walked the short distance to the camp. Mama showed our identification papers to the French gendarmes at the gate. They directed us to the visitors' center, where Papa was waiting. He swept me up in a big hug and then embraced Mama. We were so glad to be together again.

Papa showed us his living quarters in barrack number 4. Then we sat with Cousin Joseph and Papa's friends and their families in the visitors' center. Mama had made a sponge cake and brought a basket filled with some of Papa's favorite foods. While the grownups ate and talked, the children played. It seemed like a party to me, but when I looked at Mama's face, I saw that it wasn't. She remarked on how thin Papa was. "Rivelé, you worry too much," he said.

Too soon, a gendarme barked an order for all visitors to leave. I clung to Papa and wouldn't let go. Mama had to pry me loose. Papa tried to keep our farewell normal. "Rivelé," he said to Mama, "don't forget to write Abraham and ask for news of the family. And you, Isaac, try a little harder in school!" Outside the camp, Mama and I waved to Papa for the last time. He waved back from behind the barbed-wire fence until we were out of sight.

The men in barrack number 4 at Pithiviers, summer of 1941: (top) my father, Moïshé Sztrymfman, is first on the right in the back row; (bottom) my father is third from the left in the back row

PERSECUTION OF JEWS

We only made the trip to Pithiviers that once because, soon after, family visits were no longer allowed. In June of 1942, we got Papa's last letter. It ended with "We're leaving the camp in eight days. As soon as I know where we're going, I'll write. Love and kisses, Papa."

With Papa gone, things got harder. Luckily, Mama had saved some money, and we survived by living frugally. Mama bought yellow stars symbolizing the Star of David, which we were required to wear when we went out on the street. She sewed them on our coats with very fine stitches.

"Mama, why do I have to wear this star? I'm French!" I said. "You're also a Jew," she answered. "All Jews must now wear the yellow star. It's the law!" I didn't really mind at first; Marcel and all the Jewish kids wore them. I was eight years old.

But as time passed, the situation for Jews worsened. In early July, school closed for summer vacation. The government issued additional restrictions against Jews. A curfew was imposed and lists were posted specifying items that Jews were prohibited from owning. Mr. Rosenbloom took Marcel's bicycle to the police station, where it was confiscated. Mama had to turn in our radio.

One day, I asked Mama for money to go to the movies. "Why don't you go to the park with Marcel instead?" she said.

Jews were no longer permitted in movie theaters. Marcel and I went to the small park near our house where we often played. A policeman stopped us. "Can't you read?" he said, pointing to a sign. "Jews and dogs are not allowed!" And when Mama and I took the Métro, we had to ride in the last car of the train. It was reserved for Jews.

Little by little, more restrictions were enacted. Jews were not allowed to own businesses. Jews were not allowed to shop for food until after five o'clock in the evening. By then, the shelves in the stores were practically empty. But Papa had once done our Christian neighbor a favor, and she did our shopping for us.

Persecution of Jews was now official government policy. The Paris police began mass arrests, sometimes with more zeal than the Nazis. One day, when I went upstairs to play with Marcel, a neighbor told me the Rosenblooms had left. Next, we heard that several Jewish families in our building had been arrested during the night. Mama and I removed our yellow stars and stopped going outside. We hid in our apartment till that frightening morning when Mama, looking agitated, woke me. Men were yelling outside our front door. "Open the door! It's the police!" Mama put her finger to her lips, signaling me to be quiet. I was shaking with fear but made no sound. They knocked again and again and tried the door. "Open up!" But we didn't move. Finally, I heard someone say, "The concierge has the keys," and the men left.

Mama waited till the stairway was quiet before carefully opening the door. Peering out, she pulled me after her into the empty hallway and quietly locked the door behind us. Still in our nightclothes, we tiptoed noiselessly across the way to Papa's workshop. The police returned soon after, and we heard their angry shouts. "*L'appartement est vide. Les juifs sont partis!* The apartment is empty. The Jews have left." Luckily for us, they didn't know about Papa's shop.

We waited for evening and darkness before going back to our apartment to get our clothes. Mama took additional garments, her jewelry, and her money, and we returned to Papa's shop in a hurry. She packed her clothes and mine in two separate bundles and tied them with heavy twine. We slept in the shop that night, which was fortunate, for the police came back in the morning. Finding the apartment empty, they left again.

Our good neighbor brought us food and we stayed in the shop, keeping clear of the windows. After several days, Mama decided to leave. Early one morning, we tiptoed silently through the courtyard and past the apartment of the concierge. We were fortunate that the concierge didn't see us, for she hated children and Jews equally and would have gladly turned us over to the police.

We rushed across the street to 55, rue de la Fontaine au Roi, where Mama's friend Sara lived. She was married to a Christian and at that time was not yet in danger of being arrested. She had promised to help us if we needed it. Mama wanted to get to the free French zone, the part of France that wasn't under German occupation. Sara knew someone who, if paid—for it was dangerous work—would act as our guide. She took the money Mama gave her and left to make the arrangements. When she returned, it was all settled. We would be leaving early the next morning.

My mother and me, summer of 1936

Papa's last letter from Pithiviers

Mama and I go by bus to visit Papa at Pithiviers

This is Papa

A photograph of Papa and his hometown friends from Poland in front of barrack 4

Papa gives me a big hug

Papa, Mama, and I have a joyful reunion

Mama shows our identification papers to the French gendarme at Pithiviers

ARC À JEUX

SERVÉ AUX ENFANTS

ERDIT AUX JUIFS

We get off the train at a
deserted railroad station
in the middle
of the countryside

Jews are not allowed
in public parks

The camp at Pithiviers

Mama and I flee our Paris apartment

Papa waves goodbye to us from behind barbed wire

THE PASSAGE

That night, I slept in my street clothes on the living-room sofa. Mama slept in an armchair nearby. When she woke me, it was still dark. Sara was preparing snacks to send with us. I washed my face in ice-cold water at the kitchen sink. We left Sara and went out into the early morning.

The subway platform was deserted except for a cleaning person and two policemen. A train rumbled into the station, and the police watched us go aboard. The doors closed and Mama and I breathed more easily. When we stepped out into the street, it was daylight.

Mama took my hand and we hurried through the crowded railroad station to the spot where we were to meet our guide. Nazi patrols and the police were everywhere, checking people's papers, but no one stopped us. Then a man came up to us and spoke quietly to Mama. "Are you a friend of Sara's?" he asked. Mama nodded. "Follow me," he said.

He opened the door to a train compartment where an elderly couple and a young man were seated. They were making the passage, too. They looked up at us and, without saying a word, made room for Mama and me next to the open window. It was July and the day was already hot. With a sudden jolt and a deafening screech, the train moved forward. It picked up speed and we left the station in a cloud of steam. Soon, our guide and traveling companions dozed. Mama and I were hungry and shared one of the sandwiches Sara had made for us. Then Mama shut her eyes, and I looked out the window at the countryside as the train took us away from Paris.

Four hours later, we arrived at a small deserted station surrounded by farmland. Mama and I and our small group were the only passengers to leave the train. We followed our guide down a dirt road bordered by tall trees, which gave us welcome shade. We walked for a while in silence and stopped within sight of a paved road that ran at a right angle to ours. A short distance away was the line of demarcation. Beyond it was the free French zone.

The guide directed us to lie down in an irrigation ditch by the side of the road while he went ahead to make sure it was safe to proceed. We followed him with our eyes until he reached the line of demarcation. Then he turned the corner and disappeared. We waited in the ditch.

THE ARREST

First we heard shouting. Then we saw our guide running toward us, waving his arms excitedly over his head. Not far behind him came a German soldier furiously pedaling a bicycle, calling for the guide to stop. The soldier caught up with him just as he reached our hiding place. Jumping off his bicycle, the German unsheathed his bayonet, pointed his rifle at us, and ordered us onto the road with our hands over our heads. A second soldier, holding a dog by the leash, quickly joined his comrade, and they marched us to a military post nearby. There we were hustled onto a truck and driven to an ancient prison administered by the French. Orders were barked in German and French for us to climb down from the truck. As we were led through the prison gates, a terrifying vision of falling into a deep, dark hole came over me.

The doors of the prison closed behind us and day turned to night. When my eyes adjusted to the darkness, I saw that we were in a long, narrow tunnel with light at the end. The prison guards locked the six of us in one small windowless cell. There were no chairs or benches, only the stone floor strewn with straw to sit or lie upon. The straw was damp and sour-smelling. The worn cell walls were covered with scratched inscriptions made by past prisoners.

Mama and I lay down to rest. We were all stunned and no

one talked. From time to time I could hear crying in adjacent cells. I lay against Mama sheltered in her arms, thinking of Papa, Marcel, and all my friends. Mama woke me when the guards came with a watery carrot soup.

I don't remember the length of our stay, but it was at least several days. On the last day, I saw Mama take money and jewelry from her handbag and quickly hand them to one of our guards. Then she whispered the name and address of a friend in Paris to him. He wrote it down. I didn't understand why at the time.

Some time later, prison guards freed the six of us from our cell and took us with our belongings down to the other end of the tunnel and out into an immense circular courtyard, where we joined a long line of people who looked as bedraggled as we did. The line snaked around the courtyard. Shouts and cries came from the far end, and I soon saw what was causing them. Nazi officers and prison guards were separating the men from the women and children as they reached the head of the line. The men went quietly, but the women, with arms outstretched and children crying at their sides, called out hysterically to be allowed to go with their husbands. Mama and I held hands. I was scared, and I could tell Mama was, too, though she didn't say anything.

Holding a bawling toddler in his arms, the same prison guard whom Mama had given her money and jewelry to approached us. He whispered something in Mama's ear. She nodded. "Isaac," she said gently, placing my hand in his, "go with the nice man. And I don't want you to cry!" I was confused and frightened, but her voice told me that I had to try to obey her. She kissed me and her tears wet my cheek. I went quietly with the guard.

"Why isn't Mama coming?" I asked. The prison guard said nothing. "Where am I going?" "To a hospital," he answered. "Why?" "Stop asking questions!" he replied sharply.

An ambulance was parked just outside the fortress. The guard opened the back door and told me to climb in. Two girls who looked like sisters and a woman who appeared to be a nurse sat on one of the benches. After handing the toddler to the nurse, the guard passed along the piece of paper with the name and address of Mama's friend on it and shut the door. As the ambulance pulled away, I asked the nurse, "When will I see Mama?"

"I don't know," she said quietly.

"Why am I going to a hospital? I'm not sick!"

"You'll have to pretend you are," she answered. "You don't want to be deported!"

The prison in 2003

Our German captors march us to a military post

We are locked together in a small cell

Wives beg to go with their husbands

In the immense courtyard, Nazi officers separate the men from the women and children

I go with the prison guard

I feel as though
I'm falling into a
deep, dark hole

THE HOSPITAL

On our arrival at the hospital, the two girls and I were put in wheelchairs and taken to the children's ward, where we were each assigned a bed and given a hospital gown to wear. My bundle and street clothes were taken away.

I soon learned that none of the children were sick. We were all Jews who had been rescued from imminent deportation. The doctors and nurses who ran the hospital were kind to us as they kept up the pretense that we were sick. I remained there a month. Except for trips to the bathroom by wheelchair—for Germans checked the ward frequently—we were ordered to stay in bed. Mealtimes and visits by doctors and nurses broke up the daily monotony of hospital life. Sisters from a nearby convent brought us books and drawing materials.

Several times a week, a child would leave the hospital, accompanied by an adult, and another child would take his place. I didn't know where these children went, but I was happy when my turn came because I thought I would be reunited with Mama. Instead, I was handed over to a man who took me back to Paris, to a good friend of Mama's who lived in a building near ours. She half opened her front door on hearing my voice.

"Madame Ullman," said my guardian, "the boy's mother has instructed us to leave her son in your care."

"I can't take him," whispered Mama's friend. She was visibly frightened. "My husband's been arrested. It's not safe here. I'm alone with my baby. I'm sorry," and she shut her door.

My guardian didn't know what to do with me and asked me to show him where I lived. I took him to 60, rue de la Fontaine au Roi. There he left me with the concierge, who waited until he was out of sight and then chased me into the street screaming, "I won't have a Jew in my house!"

The hospital in 2003

Jacques, age 11

Danielle, age 11 months

Michel, age 14

Odette, age 7

Liliane, age 5

Adèle, age 2, and her sister, Paulette, 9

Edgar, age 7

Jean, age 6

Claude, age 14

I am taken to a hospital and hidden with other Jewish children in the children's ward

Nicole, age 13

Denise, age 3

Pauline, age 2, and her brother, Charles, 10

Francis, age 8

Germaine, age 2

David, age 11, and his brother, Albert, 13

Lucienne, age 8

Marcel, age 9

Louise, age 3½

HÉNA

I sat on the sidewalk in front of 60, rue de la Fontaine au Roi crying, wondering where I could go. Who would help me? It was dusk when a woman stopped and questioned me. In thickly accented French, similar to Mama's, she asked where I lived. I pointed to our windows. She asked where my mama and papa were. "I don't know!" I answered. She asked my name and understood that I was a Jew. "I'm a Jew, too," she whispered. "My name is Héna." I stopped crying. She wiped my tears with a handkerchief and took me home with her.

Héna lived in a small three-room apartment. She sat me down in the kitchen and heated some soup. After dinner, I helped her open the living-room couch to make a bed. She gave me a pair of pajamas that were much too large. I put them on. "They belonged to my son," she said, laughing. I was tired and fell asleep quickly.

When I woke up in the morning, she wasn't there. I found a note on the kitchen table that said she had gone to work. She left me a hard-boiled egg and a glass of milk for breakfast. There was smoked ham, an apple, and some bread for my lunch. The note warned me not to go out. "Stay in the apartment, and don't answer or open the door for anyone. Héna."

I had never been left alone before and at first didn't know what to do with myself. Then I found a pencil and paper in the living room. I sat by the window and drew while waiting for Héna's return. I drew the buildings across the way. I drew pictures of Mama and Papa and all my friends. I drew everything I saw in the room.

At dinner Héna told me that she, like Mama and Papa, had emigrated from Poland. She had a grandson my age and a granddaughter a year younger. They were hidden with their parents somewhere in France. She also had a sister who lived in a village outside Paris.

Héna and her grandchildren, 1934   *Héna's hidden grandchildren, 1942*

11.me ARRt

60 RUE DE LA FONTAINE au ROI

I sit on the sidewalk in front of 60, rue de la Fontaine au Roi, crying

"I can't take him," says Mama's friend. "I'm alone with my baby. I'm sorry."

Héna takes me home with her

I draw pictures of
Mama and Papa

The concierge chases
me into the street
screaming, "I won't
have a Jew
in my house!"

Héna tells me she is a Jew,
which makes me feel better

PONTAULT-COMBAULT

I left with Héna in the morning. She was taking me to her sister. The French underground had blown up the railroad bridge at Nogent, and our train had to take a roundabout route to reach Pontault-Combault. Héna's sister, Madame Laks, and her husband were outside their house tending their garden when we arrived. Food was scarce during the war, so people in the countryside grew their own fruits and vegetables.

Madame Laks wiped her hands and embraced Héna. The sisters spoke Yiddish together. "Who's the boychick?" she asked. Héna leaned close to her sister and whispered, "His name is Isaac. I found him on the street. His parents have been arrested and deported. I'd like to hide him with good people till his parents return."

Héna placed me with the Merciers, an older couple who had made it known that they wanted to take in a child to add to their income. On the way to the Merciers', Héna changed my name from Isaac to Jean—"a good French name," she said. I was to call her "Mémé," for Grandma, and never, never tell anyone that we were Jews.

MADAME MERCIER

Madame Mercier frightened me the first time I saw her. She was dressed in somber clothes, and a green ointment covered her face—evidently a cure for some skin ailment. Her husband sat like a stone at the kitchen table, eating; a black hound lay on the tiled floor by his feet. The animal growled as we entered. Monsieur Mercier kicked it and the growling stopped.

"Jean, say goodbye to your grandmother," said Madame Mercier brusquely. She and Héna had just agreed on the amount of money Madame Mercier would receive for keeping me. I cried myself to sleep that night, praying for Mama and Papa to come quickly and take me away. I wished I had never been born a Jew.

I stayed with the Merciers for two months. Every night I went to bed hungry. To make certain I didn't steal any food, Madame Mercier locked me in my room whenever she and her husband went out. One Sunday morning, I woke up with sharp hunger pangs. I knew I would find something to eat in the kitchen, but the Merciers had gone to church and my door was locked. I decided to take a chance. The top half of the door had four panes of glass, and the pane nearest the doorknob was missing. By climbing onto a chair, I could reach through the hole to the key, which had been left in the keyhole on the other side. Turning it slowly and carefully, I opened the door. Cautiously,

37

with the dog watching every move I made, I tiptoed into the kitchen. I was about to grab some bread when Madame Mercier returned. "I know how to deal with a thief!" she screamed, and locked me in my room again. This time she put the key in her pocket.

In the coming days, my misery deepened when my scalp began to itch. I scratched and scratched, but the itching only got worse. Soon ugly sores appeared. I kept on scratching; then pus oozed out. When Héna came to see me, she was horrified by my condition. "I should have come sooner!" she lamented, and took me from the Merciers. As we walked away, she explained that Madame Laks and her husband had been afraid to leave their house, for fear of being arrested, and that it was only recently that her sister learned from a neighbor what had happened to me.

Héna holding one of her great-grandsons, 1961

Héna with another great-grandson and her sister, Madame Laks, 1962

Monsieur Mercier

Madame Mercier
locks me in my room

Héna takes me away
from the Merciers

Madame Mercier frightens me.
She is dressed in somber clothes,
and a green ointment
covers her face

Madame Mercier counts
the money Héna gave
her to keep me

"I know how to deal
with a thief!" screams
Madame Mercier

BANQUE DE FRANCE
CENT FRANCS
100
100

Slowly and carefully,
I open the door

I wish I had
never been
born a Jew

Each night, I pray
for Mama and Papa
to come

I am given rutabaga
in water for supper

MADAME DEVOLDER

"A good clean bath and a hard scrubbing with warm water and soap," said Madame Devolder, "and in a few weeks you will see, the sores on Jean's scalp will be gone!" Madame Devolder had just told Héna she would look after me.

A widow, Madame Devolder lived in a small house surrounded by woods in the village of Pontault, a twenty-minute walk from Héna's sister. She came from the northern part of Belgium and spoke with a light Flemish accent. She was tall and strong, with a deep voice, a hearty laugh, and a kind face. I liked her right away. Madame Devolder disinfected my clothes, shaved my head, and scrubbed it hard with soap and water. And, as she had predicted, in a few weeks the sores on my scalp had healed. She hid me through the final war years, treating me like a son. I became Jean Devolder.

Life with Madame Devolder soon settled into a daily work routine. Though calm and peaceful, it was still difficult. We lived on a shoestring and often went hungry. But no matter how little food there was, she shared it equally with me. We worked hard, and there was plenty to do—cleaning the outhouse, washing laundry by hand (there was no washing machine), toiling in our small vegetable garden, and many other chores.

In May, clusters of tiny wild strawberries sprouted in the countryside. Blood red and easily spotted under green patches of foliage, they satisfied my hunger for something sweet. In the summer months after the harvest, we gleaned wheat remaining in Farmer Grégoire's field. In the fall, we dug for potatoes he had left in the ground. He also let us take apples that had fallen from the trees in his orchard. This helped us during lean times.

One day, Farmer Grégoire gave me a baby rabbit. Madame Devolder said I could keep it, but she reminded me that when the rabbit grew up, we would have to eat it. I didn't want to think about that. For the time being I was happy; I had something that was mine to love and care for. I named my rabbit Rose.

Early the next morning, Madame Devolder sent me to Farmer Grégoire to fill our milk jug. The road to the farm led past an ancient stone wall that enclosed the town cemetery. A narrow strip of grass dotted with daisies and bright red poppies ran the length of the wall. I heard an animal's shrieks and then saw Farmer Grégoire in his courtyard arguing with a German officer. Two soldiers had cornered a pig and were struggling to get it into the back of their truck. They were attached to the occupation troops who had made the Château of Combault their headquarters. As I watched in silence, the officer's greenish gray military uniform and black boots brought back terrifying memories of the prison courtyard where I was separated from Mama. With the pig finally captured, the officer gave the order to leave. "*Sales voleurs!* Dirty thieves!" Farmer Grégoire shouted as the truck roared away.

MY FRIENDS

Madame Devolder enrolled me in the village school. To get there, I cut through the woods to Farmer Grégoire's field. There I would meet André Grégoire and walk the rest of the way with him. He was the farmer's son and, though he was two years older, sat next to me in class. He was chubby and a little slow-witted, but gentle and generous. Once, when I'd pulled up some carrots from his father's field, he offered to trade the piece of lard he was eating. "Jean, my lard for your carrot!" Because he often said silly things, the other children made fun of him.

Victor Feldman sat several desks behind me in class. He had curly blond hair and was a year younger. I found out that he lived with his father on avenue des Marguerites. I didn't learn more, for Victor didn't talk much. After several weeks, I noticed that he'd stopped coming to class. When I mentioned it to Madame Devolder, she said, "Jean, the police found out that Victor and his father are Jews. They arrested them and both were deported!"

Another classmate, Pierre Allazetta, was a dwarf. He lived with his mother and two sisters in the village. His father was a prisoner of war in a camp in Germany. Pierre always made me laugh, especially when he imitated Fernandel, a movie actor and comic. Pierre hoped to become one himself when he grew up. André, Pierre, and I became best friends.

Since we had no real toys, we played with things we found. A broken-down cardboard box or an old discarded can were fun to kick around. I taught my friends to play marbles. And Pierre taught us the game of knucklebone. The butcher had given him the five bones for free. The idea is to throw all five bones on the ground. Then throw one into the air, grab a bone from the ground, and catch the airborne bone on the way down with the same hand, without touching any of the others. I never could beat Pierre.

Once, on a day off from school, my friends and I decided to go to the open-air market. A shortcut ran through a wooded property. It was Pierre who first suggested we use it. None of us had ever taken it before.

"The path?" André and I said, hesitating.

"Scared?" said Pierre.

"Of course not!" we replied bravely. I took a deep breath, and pushed warily forward onto the narrow dirt path. It was dark and spooky. We were jumpy and spoke in whispers. Every little noise startled us. When a rabbit leaped out of the underbrush, my friends and I darted to the other side in a hurry. "I wasn't scared," Pierre said in a plucky voice. André and I didn't believe him. We never took the shortcut again. There was no telling where the enemy might be hiding.

Jean Devolder

Cours Moyen 2ème année

Lundi 20 septembre

Operations

```
        7 8 6
  1 7 6       × 1 9 4
× 6 0 9       ─────────
─────────     3 1 4 4
  1 5 8 4     7 0 7 4
1 0 5 6       7 8 6
─────────     ─────────
1 0 7 1 8 4   1 5 2 1 ?
```

no262

In school, I write with pen and ink, which leaves smudges on my fingers

Pierre, André, and me on the way to school

Madame Devolder shaves my head and scrubs and washes me

Pierre's knucklebones

Playing knucklebone

The Château de Candalle of Pontault and our school

Teachers lived on the second floor of the schoolhouse, and classrooms were on the first

The Grégoire farm

Farmer Grégoire with his horse, Gamin

German soldiers take Farmer Grégoire's pig

The Pontault church

Father Paul Botz on his motor bicycle

LIFE WAS HARSH

One afternoon, I came home from school and found Madame Devolder holding my rabbit, now full-grown. Madame Devolder had a determined expression on her face. I broke into tears. "No, Madame Devolder! Please don't hurt Rose! I love her!" I pleaded in vain. It was wartime. There wasn't enough food, and we had to eat.

Life was harsh, for everything was scarce. In winter, Madame Devolder and I made trips to the sawmill and filled our wheelbarrow with wood shavings we collected from the floor. Firewood was expensive and the wood shavings were free. They kept us from freezing.

I came home from school one day feeling sick and soon developed a bad chest cold and heavy cough. To treat the cold, Madame Devolder applied hot mustard plasters on my chest. The mustard had a sharp, powerful odor and Madame Devolder was careful not to burn me. When the cough persisted, she pressed six cupping glasses to my bare back. The glasses made a popping sound when removed and left reddish purple circles on my skin. The mustard plaster and cupping glass were common remedies for chest colds at the time. When Madame Devolder fell ill, it was my turn to treat her, for we didn't have the money to spend on doctors.

The kitchen was the warmest room in the house during the

cold winter months. We sat around the table, where I did my homework under the watchful eye of Madame Devolder while she mended clothes. I didn't have many, so when my pants or shirts wore thin, she patched them. When the heels and soles of my shoes needed repair, she took them to Monsieur Lazucatto, the shoemaker, who replaced them with wood because he couldn't get leather. Walking on these stiff soles took some getting used to.

After dinner, Madame Devolder and I played cards till the fire in the kitchen stove died out. And then it was bedtime. Darkness fell quickly in winter. There were often power failures, and we used candles sparingly by going to bed early. Shivering, I'd slide under the blankets in Madame Devolder's bed to get warm.

In late 1943, we began noticing airplanes flying high over Pontault. My friends and I counted them, "One, two, three . . ." They flew in groups. ". . . twelve, thirteen, fourteen . . ." They kept on coming. ". . . eighteen, nineteen, twenty, twenty-one . . ." I asked Madame Devolder about them. "Americans!" she answered. "On their way to bomb Germany!"

On important religious holidays I went to church with Madame Devolder. The Grégoire and Allazetta families went, too. There were two Catholic churches in Pontault-Combault, but only one priest. Father Paul Botz conducted services at both. As soon as he'd finished one, he'd jump on his old motor bicycle and ride very fast to get to the other church.

There wasn't much to celebrate for the winter holidays. Still, we went into the woods and cut down a small evergreen. We dragged it home and placed it in the kitchen. Madame Devolder brought out her precious Christmas ornaments, kept with great care in two beautiful old metal cookie boxes. One of the boxes held fragile glass balls with Christmas scenes embedded in them. In the other I found garlands and a shiny star made of bits of aluminum foil saved from wrappers.

"Christmas is a very special holiday for me, Jean. It brings back so many fond memories of my family when I was a little girl growing up in Belgium." I had never heard Madame Devolder speak so freely, and it surprised me. "Don't forget to shine your shoes before you put them under the tree!" she said. It was Christmas Eve of 1943. I put my shined shoes under the tree before going to bed. I was too old to believe in Santa, but I couldn't wait until morning to see what Madame Devolder had left in my shoe. It was a woolen scarf she'd knitted. And in the other, an added surprise: a beautiful orange. I had not eaten one since early in the war.

Sometimes, days went by when I didn't think about the war or Mama and Papa. On the first of April, André, Pierre, and I pinned small cutout paper fish on our classmates' backs without their knowing it. We laughed and shouted "April Fool's Day!" till we discovered that paper fish had also been pinned on us.

On the first of May, which was a holiday, Madame Devolder and I picked lilies of the valley in the woods behind the house. Madame Devolder looked pretty in her spring dress as we stood across from the graveyard selling bouquets of flowers to passersby to make a little extra money.

Héna had stopped coming to see me. We didn't know why. I learned later that she had been summoned to the police station and was on the verge of being deported when a policeman singled her out and told her to leave the station. After that, Héna, too, went into hiding.

Me as Jean Devolder (front row, second from left), standing between my friends Pierre and André at the village school, 1944

THE LIBERATION

News was censored. What little we heard came from neighbors who had radios. I was helping Madame Devolder in the garden when Pierre's mother came running. *"Les Américains ont débarqué sur les plages de Normandie!* The Americans have landed on the beaches of Normandy!" She was crying, but her tears were tears of joy. Madame Devolder turned to me, smiling. "Jean," she said, "you'll be seeing your parents soon!"

Greeted by the sound of church bells, bouquets of flowers, and the singing of the French national anthem, the Americans liberated Pontault-Combault in August 1944. It seemed that the whole village had turned out to welcome our liberators. We waved French and American flags as the column of tanks rumbled into the village square. When the tanks stopped in front of the town hall for a short while, André, Pierre, and I got to climb up on one. The column moved on, and my friends and I ran alongside.

The Americans were passing Héna's sister's house when they stopped again. A soldier jumped down from his tank. Proud to be near an American, we followed him as he walked over to Madame Laks, who was in her front garden. Pointing to the water pump, the soldier began to say something. She quickly understood that he was asking for water and, in her excitement, spoke several words of Yiddish. The soldier smiled. "My name is

Epstein! I'm a Jew. And I speak Yiddish." Madame Laks was over-joyed. "You're welcome to the water," she said. "Take all you want."

My friends and I took turns filling the soldiers' canteens, and the Americans thanked us with chewing gum. It was the first time I chewed gum. Then they climbed aboard their tanks, and André, Pierre, and I followed the convoy as far as the railroad station, where we left them. On the way back, we joined a group of villagers gathered around a bullet-riddled German car that lay on its side in the road. We learned that the car, carrying SS officers fleeing the advancing Allies, had taken a wrong turn and met the Americans head-on. Fascinated, I watched a dying German take his last breath.

My two friends came to see me off when I left Pontault-Combault in the spring of 1945. Pierre gave me his knuckle-bones as a going-away present and André parted with his sling-shot. Madame Devolder dried her eyes with her handkerchief. "Jean," she said, embracing me, "I'll miss you!" As I walked away with Héna, a part of me felt sad.

Madame Devolder and I fill our wheelbarrow with wood shavings at the sawmill

1943 Janvier 1943

The Pontault church

Madame Devolder's house

On April Fool's Day, my friends and I pin paper fish cutouts on people's backs

1943 Avril 1943

Helping Madame Devolder in her garden

1943 Mai 1943

On the first of May, a workers' holiday, we sell lilies of the valley to passersby

The outdoor market

Farmer Grégoire's wheat field

Madame Devolder and I dig up potatoes left in the ground after the potato harvest

1943 *Septembre 1943*

The village square

1943 *Décembre 1943*

The railroad station

Celebrating Christmas with Madame Devolder

The town cemetery

1944 *Août 1944*

In August 1944, the Americans liberate Pontault-Combault

The school

LES BUISSONS

Héna placed me in Les Buissons, a temporary home for Jewish children who had been orphaned or separated from their families during the war. It was housed in a modest mansion on the outskirts of the city of Le Mans. I was not happy there. I disliked the regimented life, the communal living, and the strict discipline imposed by Serge, the autocratic director of the home.

Still, much of what he did for us was good. He taught us to appreciate classical music and great literature. We learned about Jewish culture, and I relearned Yiddish, which I had seldom heard during all those years in hiding. We were given piano lessons and sang Jewish songs—the same songs Mama had once sung to me. We went on frequent hikes, learned new games and folk dances, and put on plays, which we performed for visitors during the holidays.

At first the meals at the home consisted of cauliflower in the morning, again at lunch, and for supper, too. And sometimes red beets, to vary the menu. Thanks to money raised by Jews in the United States, our food improved later on. Each day before lunch, we had to swallow a spoonful of cod-liver oil to remedy a vitamin deficiency brought on by malnutrition during the war. To kill the odious taste, we'd put a pinch of salt on a piece of bread and keep it at the ready, then hold our noses as we quickly swallowed the cod-liver oil, and, just as fast, follow it with the bread. But the fishy aftertaste remained in our mouths.

Jewish American soldiers based in Le Mans often came to visit us. They brought us canned goods, as well as chocolate, candy, and chewing gum. They also drove us into town in their army trucks so we could go to the movies. After seeing *Robin Hood,* my friends and I made bows and arrows. I had two adolescent loves at the home, a secret crush on a girl named Charlotte, who had beautiful eyes—one brown, the other black—and a love for a snowy white puppy that had been given to the shelter by a neighboring farmer.

School was a half hour away by foot. Coming home took longer because the road was uphill. We walked in a group, and Frida, a counselor, usually accompanied us each way on her bicycle. She had a number tattooed on her arm. We all knew she had gotten it in a concentration camp. She never talked about it. I remember local children sometimes throwing stones at us as we made our way to or from school. We didn't like it, but we had lived through so much worse. We could put up with this. But one day when I was playing with classmates in the schoolyard, two older boys called me a "dirty Jew!" The principal overheard them and warned them that they would be expelled if they made anti-Semitic slurs again. Suddenly we were being protected. The war was over.

One Sunday, families and guests came from Paris to celebrate the Jewish holiday Purim with us. In the afternoon, on the grassy lawn under tall oak trees, we sang for the visitors and performed a traditional play, dating back many years. It tells the

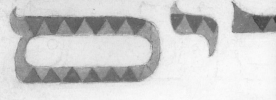

פורים

Purim Purim Purim Purim Purim

At Purim, we eat Hamantashen, little three-cornered cakes filled with poppy seeds

Children at Les

Charlotte is the beautiful Esther

They rattle noisemakers, called the ground each time the name

Mordecai tells Esther of a plot against the King

Purim celebrates the Haman, as recorded

פורים

Purim Purim Purim Purim Purim Purim

Buissons put on the Purim play

"graggers," and stamp their feet on
of the wicked Haman is mentioned

Gragger

I play
the wise
Mordecai

King Ahasuerus orders the wicked
Haman to lead Mordecai, riding the
King's horse, throughout the city

downfall of the wicked
in the book of Esther

story of the king's minister, the evil Haman, scheming the destruction of the Jewish people of Persia, who escape through the intervention of God, the bravery of Queen Esther, and the wisdom of her uncle Mordecai. Charlotte played Queen Esther and I played the wise old Mordecai. Afterward the chef, Monsieur Pierre, and his wife, Madame Olga, brought out a large cake baked in the shape of the mansion, with a shiny sugar crown on top.

In our room upstairs that night, with the light out and the door shut, my friends Carol, Victor, Vladeck, Jean, Louis Berman, and I chatted. We laughed at the practical jokes we had played on the older girls, and at the same time wondered what had happened to the sugar crown that had adorned Monsieur Pierre's cake that afternoon. It had mysteriously disappeared.

"Serge ate it," Carol whispered in the dark.

The door of our room flew open, and in the doorway stood the director. I had never seen him look so angry. It was our bad luck that Serge, who walked the halls at night listening to make certain we were all asleep, pressed an ear against our door just as Carol made his statement. Carol explained that it was just a joke, but Serge didn't see it that way. "Everybody downstairs in the dining hall!" He was raging mad. Going from room to room, he woke all the children and ordered them to the dining hall as well. The little ones, not fully awake, had to be carried in our arms.

Serge kept candy and chocolate, donated by the American

soldiers, under lock and key in a large cupboard at one corner of the dining hall. Except for moonlight filtering through the windows, the room was dark when we walked in. We went to our tables and waited silently. Serge unlocked the cupboard—he always carried the key in his pocket—took out the sweets, and began distributing them to us. "So I ate the crown!" he fumed. "No one leaves the room until all the candy and chocolate are eaten."

It was late, and no one had any real appetite for candy, but we dutifully began eating. After an hour, Serge allowed the youngest children to go back to bed. But Carol, Victor, Vladeck, Jean, Louis Berman, and I were made to stay.

"I hate him," said Carol back in our room, and we all fell asleep.

As time passed, I learned of the Nazi death camps. Still, I clung to the hope of being reunited with Mama and Papa. But as the weeks, months, and years passed, and one by one my friends left the home to be reunited with family, often a single parent and Holocaust survivor, my hope faded. And I grew angry that not one of those lucky children was me.

Then in the spring of 1948 I learned that a Jewish couple in America wanted to bring me to the United States and adopt me. "Isaac," said Héna, "this will be a very good thing for you!" I wasn't so sure, but I had no choice.

In 1946, we pose for a photograph
on the front porch of Les Buissons

I hold on to my puppy
to keep him from
scampering off

Frida tries to teach me
to play the piano,
with little success

Vladeck and I
paint Snow White
and the seven dwarfs
after seeing the movie

As time passes, my hope of being reunited with Mama and Papa fades

Jewish American soldiers drive us into town to see a movie

We perform "The Cobbler and the Financier," a fable by La Fontaine

SAVETIER

Frida conducts the chorus

LEAVING FOR AMERICA

Monsieur Pierre and his wife baked a cake for my going-away party. Before leaving for America, I went to visit 60, rue de la Fontaine au Roi. I walked past the apartment of the new concierge and made my way to the courtyard. It was smaller than I remembered. I looked up at our windows, the ones in the bedroom and living room that faced the courtyard. I climbed the stairs that Mama and I had fled down the morning the police came to arrest us. I hesitated for a moment at the front door of the old apartment, my heart pounding. Then I took the three flights of stairs to the Rosenblooms'. Marcel and his parents were there. Through sheer luck they had survived the Holocaust. I stayed awhile, and before I left, Madame Rosenbloom gave me a photograph of Mama and Papa, looking young and happy, smiling into the camera.

On November 1, 1948, I boarded a plane for the United States. I was fifteen years old and on my way to a new life. As I said goodbye to Héna, the image of Papa standing behind barbed wire at Pithiviers waving goodbye to Mama and me flashed in front of my eyes. I felt the wetness of Mama's tears on my cheek. Of my entire family—four grandparents, many uncles, aunts, and cousins—only one cousin, one uncle, and I survived.

The children and staff of Les Buissons, 1947

Les Buissons, 1948 (I am the third boy on the right)

Monsieur Pierre, the chef,
and his wife, Olga

Monsieur Pierre bakes a cake
for my going-away party

Héna says that going
to America will be a
very good thing for me

Les Buissons,
the children's home

Everyone bids me
"Bon Voyage"

AMÉRIQUE

Bon

Isaac e

T

OCÉAN AT

Voyage

...ymfman

...IA

...ANTIQUE

FRANCE

I see my friend
Marcel Rosenbloom

RUE
DE LA
FONTA...
AU R...
60

I visit 60, rue de la
Fontaine au Roi
before leaving for
the United States
of America

As I board the plane for the United States of America, the image of Papa standing behind barbed wire at Pithiviers waving goodbye to Mama and me flashes before my eyes, and I feel the wetness of Mama's tears on my cheek

AFTERWORD

The Nazis and their French collaborators kept meticulous records of their crimes during the war. It is recorded that Moszek Sztrymfman,* my father, left Pithiviers for Auschwitz with convoy number 4, on June 25, 1942, together with 998 other men between the ages of thirty-one and forty-two. And that fifty-one of them seem to have survived after the war. My father was not among them. Rywka Sztrymfman,* my mother, left Pithiviers for Auschwitz with convoy number 24, on August 26, 1942, together with 947 other deportees. According to the records, twenty-three survived. My mother was not one of them.

In 1952, I was officially adopted by Meyer and Bella Millman and took their name. At first it was difficult to adjust to a new country and accept complete strangers as parents. In time, with help from the Millmans, who were patient and loving, I did. They sent me to school and I finished my education. After college, I was drafted into the American army, became a citizen, and was sent to Europe. On leave, I visited Héna and her family, and renewed my ties with her granddaughter, Jeanine, whom I had met once before when she was twelve and I thirteen. This time we fell in love. After my discharge, she joined me in the United States and we were married. Héna was overjoyed.

---

* I have referred to my parents by their familiar names, Moïshé and Rivelé, throughout this book.

After the war, Héna left Paris for Combault to be near her sister. Some years later, my wife and I returned to France with our two little boys to visit the family, and at the first opportunity, accompanied by Héna, we went to see Madame Devolder. She was keeping a young Jewish child, not hidden, as I was, but in need of Madame Devolder's kindness and care. Ours was a happy reunion.

Today I am at peace with the past. Yet I cannot forget it, for the past is my parents.

My parents, Moïshé and Rivelé Sztrymfman

ACKNOWLEDGMENTS

I want to acknowledge the one hundred and sixty students and their teachers of the Dag Hammarskjold Middle School in East Brunswick, New Jersey, who wrote to thank me for visiting their school and speaking of my Holocaust experience. Their letters encouraged me to write *Hidden Child*.

I want to acknowledge the following people for their patience in supplying some answers to my questions during my research for *Hidden Child*: Joseph and Yvette Nisenman, Jean Sztulman, Jean Maslo, Victor Flandre, Emile Papiernik, Fernande and Lucien Kletzkine, Germaine and Léon Kletzkine, and Paulette Libeskind. I want to thank Michel Villard and Rémy Rebeyrotte, the mayor of Autun, France, for allowing me to visit the prison where my mother and I were held.

I also want to thank Katarzyna Nowak of the Auschwitz-Birkenau Museum for the research and discovery in its archives of my father's death certificate, dated February 16, 1943, Auschwitz.

It was in Serge Klarsfeld's *Le Mémorial de la Déportation des Juifs de France* ("Memorial to the Jews Deported from France") that I found the dates and numbers of the convoys that transported my father and mother to Auschwitz, where both perished.

And my heartfelt thanks to the family friend who rescued

our photo albums after my mother and I fled Paris and who gave them to me when I came out of hiding. The photos reproduced here are from that collection.

My sincere gratitude to my editor, Frances Foster, for her kind guidance throughout *Hidden Child*.

Copyright © 2005 by Isaac Millman
Distributed in Canada by Douglas & McIntyre Publishing Group
Printed and bound in China by South China Co. Ltd.
Designed by Barbara Grzeslo
First edition, 2005
1   3   5   7   9   10   8   6   4   2

www.fsgkidsbooks.com

Library of Congress Cataloging-in-Publication Data
Millman, Isaac.
   Hidden child / Isaac Millman.
      p. cm.
   Summary: The author details his difficult experiences as a young Jewish child living
in Nazi-occupied France during the 1940s.
   ISBN-13: 978-0-374-33071-2
   ISBN-10: 0-374-33071-9
   1. Millman, Isaac—Juvenile literature.   2. Jewish children in the Holocaust—
France—Biography—Juvenile literature.   3. Jews—France—Biography—Juvenile
literature.   4. Holocaust, Jewish (1939–1945)—France—Personal narratives—Juvenile
literature.   5. France—Biography—Juvenile literature.   [1. Millman, Isaac.   2. Jews—
France—Biography.   3. Holocaust, Jewish (1939–1945)—France.]   I. Title.

DS135.F9M576 2005
940.53'18'092—dc22
[B]

                                                            2003060688